The MAILBOX®

WONDER. DRAW. TELL!

77 storytelling opportunities for kindergartners

- Sparks curiosity and creativity
- Encourages communication
- Builds vocabulary
- Develops writing skills
- Supports popular teaching themes

Capture the unique ideas of every child!

Managing Editor: Lynn Drolet

Editorial Team: Becky S. Andrews, Diane Badden, Kimberley Bruck, Karen A. Brudnak, Pam Crane, Sarah Foreman, Pierce Foster, Tazmen Hansen, Marsha Heim, Lori Z. Henry, Troy Lawrence, Debra Liverman, Kitty Lowrance, Brenda Miner, Jennifer Nunn, Mark Rainey, Greg D. Rieves, Hope Rodgers, Rebecca Saunders, Donna K. Teal, Rachael Traylor, Sharon M. Tresino, Zane Williard

www.themailbox.com

Printed in the United States
10 9 8 7 6 5 4 3 2 1

HPS 215493

Table of Contents

What's Inside

77 fun ways for little ones to wonder, draw, and tell!

A label that shows the time of year and theme

A question that invites wonder

Name_____

Look Who's Sharing!

Spring
Bunnies

Wonder Who will get the carrot?

Draw

An illustration that encourages creative thinking

Space for a child to draw his or her ideas

Tell _____

Space for a child to write

Name

4

Lots of Apples

Wonder What will happen next?

Draw

Tell

That's a Plan!

Wonder How will the fox get an apple?

Draw

Tell _

_ _

_ _

Name _____

A Sweet Treat

Wonder Who will eat the apple pie?

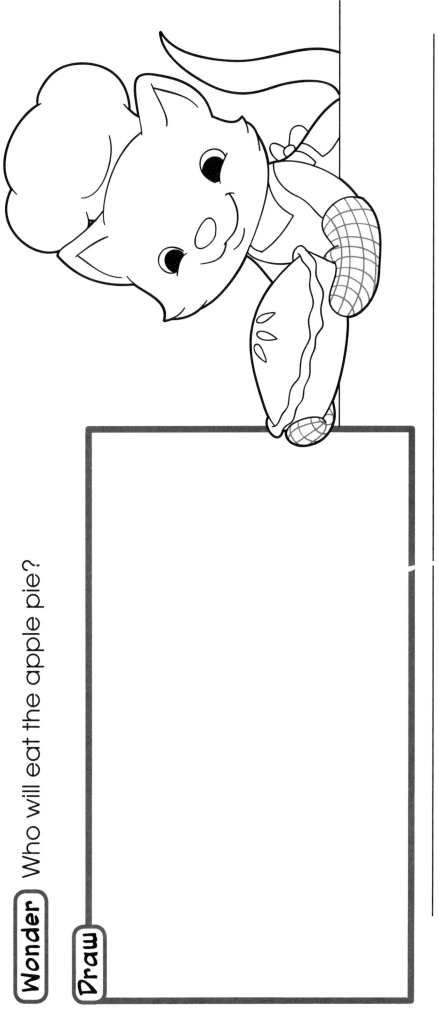

Draw

Tell

Name

A Breezy Ride

Wonder What will the leaf land on?

Draw

Tell

Fall
Leaves

Search and Find

Wonder What is the squirrel looking for?

Draw

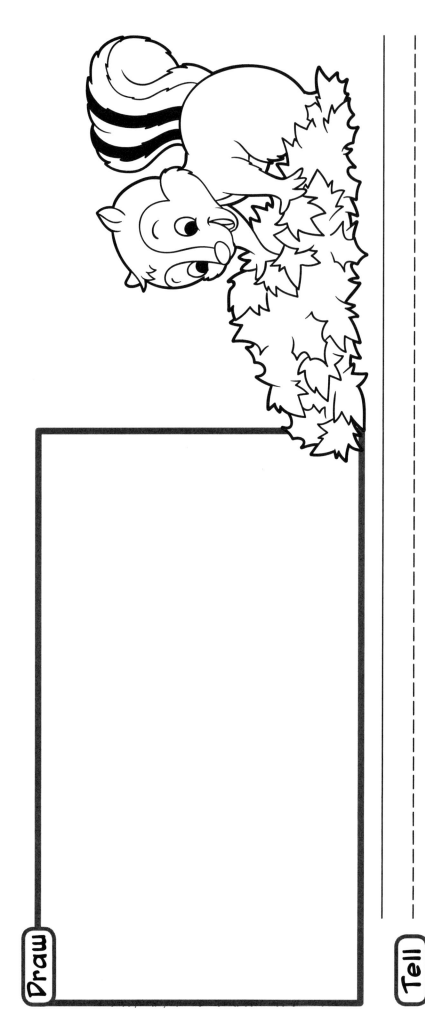

Tell

Name _____

Fall
Leaves

Pile 'em Up!

Wonder Who will rake the leaves?

Draw

Tell

- -

_____

- -

_____

- -

_____

Peekaboo!

Wonder What is hiding behind the pumpkin?

Draw

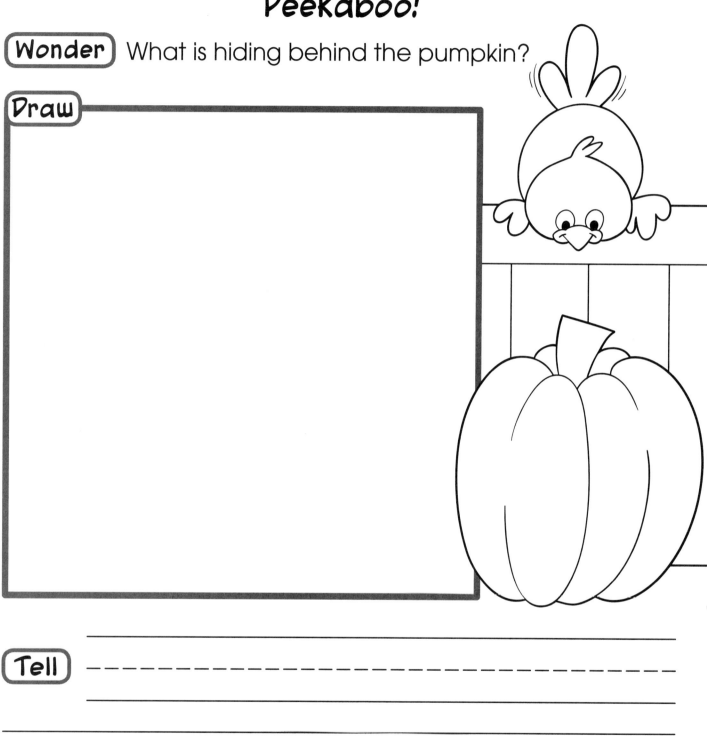

Tell _____

_____

_____

_____

_____

Wonder, Draw, Tell! • ©The Mailbox® Books • TEC61274

Visitors at Night

Wonder What visits the pumpkin patch at night?

Draw

Tell

Name _____

It's a Mystery

Wonder What happened to the farmer's pumpkins?

Draw

Tell

Name _____

Scooping Seeds

Wonder What will the raccoon do next?

Draw

Tell _____

Wonder, Draw, Tell! • ©The Mailbox® Books • TEC61274

Name

Give Thanks

Wonder Who are **you** thankful for?

Draw

Tell

14

Name _____

A Yummy Treat

Wonder What smells so good?

Draw

Tell _____

_____

Name

16

Happy Thanksgiving!

Wonder What would be the best Thanksgiving Day dinner?

Draw

Tell

Name

A Holiday Game

Wonder Who is playing with the dreidel?

Draw

Tell

Wonder, Draw, Tell! • ©The Mailbox® Books • TEC61274

A Busy Elf

Wonder What will the elf make?

Draw

Tell

Wonder, Draw, Tell! • ©The Mailbox® Books • TEC61274

Name

A Lively Gift

Wonder What is moving in the sack?

Draw

Tell

The Best Present Ever!

Wonder What does the moose see?

Draw

Tell _____

_____

_____

_____

_____

Wonder, Draw, Tell! • ©The Mailbox® Books • TEC61274

Oh, Happy Day!

Wonder Who gave the dog a bone?

Draw

Tell _____

_ _ _ _ _ _ _ _ _ _ _

_ _ _ _ _ _ _ _ _ _ _

Whoosh!

Wonder What made the candles go out?

Draw

Tell

_ _ _ _ _ _ _ _ _ _ _ _ _ _ _ _ _ _ _ _

It's Cold Outside!

Wonder What will you wear to play in the snow?

Draw

Tell

_____
_ _ _ _ _ _ _ _ _ _ _ _ _ _ _ _ _
_____
_____
_ _ _ _ _ _ _ _ _ _ _ _ _ _ _ _ _
_____
_____
_ _ _ _ _ _ _ _ _ _ _ _ _ _ _ _ _
_____

Whee!

Wonder Who will go down the hill next?

Draw

Tell

Name_____

A Friend for Penguin

Wonder What will the snowman look like?

Draw

Tell _____

_____

_____

_____

_____

_____

Name _____

Snow Day

Wonder What do you do when it snows?

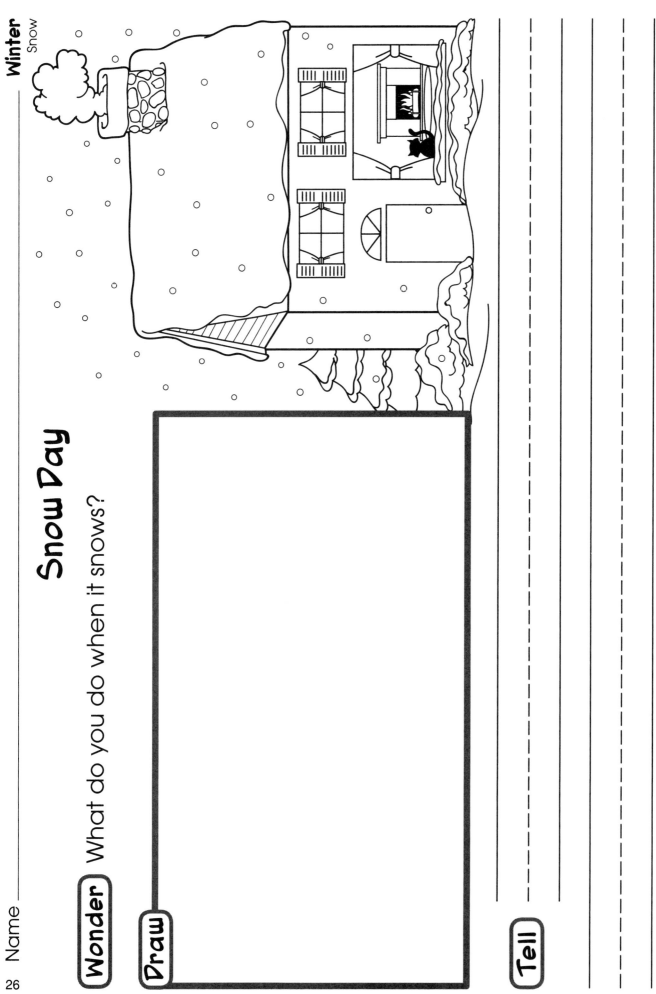

Draw

Tell

Name_____

For You!

Wonder What is the lion hiding behind its back?

Draw

Tell

- -

- -

- -

Skunk's Sweetheart

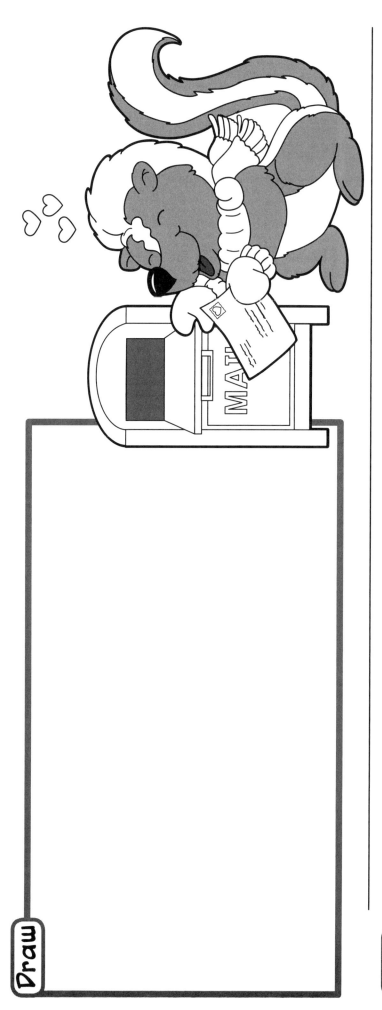

Wonder Who will get the letter?

Draw

Tell

- -

- -

Made With Love

Wonder What will the porcupine paint?

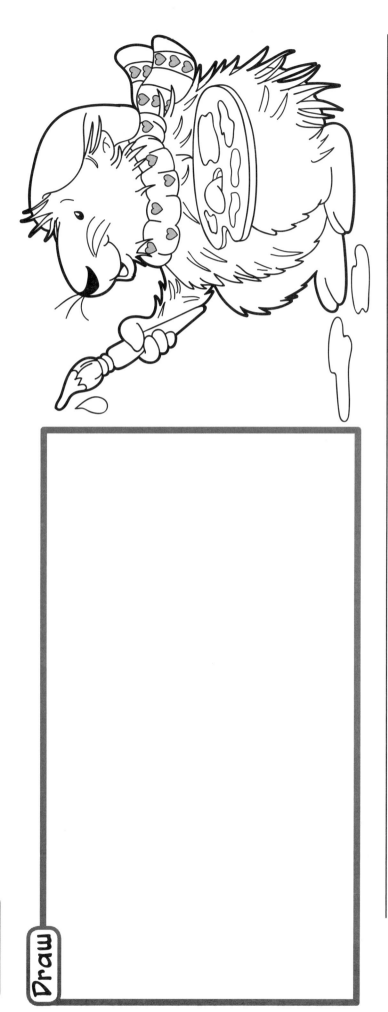

Draw

Tell

Name _____

30

Handmade Heart

Wonder Who would **you** make a heart for?

Draw

Tell

Winter
Friendship

Name _____

Time For a Photo!

Wonder What friend would be in the photo with you?

Draw

Best Friends

Tell

Name _____

32

Fun With My Friend

Wonder What would you do with a friend?

Draw

Tell

Rainy Day Fun

Wonder What likes the rain?

Draw

Tell

34

Windy Day

Wonder Who is flying the kite?

Draw

Tell

Name _____

Perfect Weather

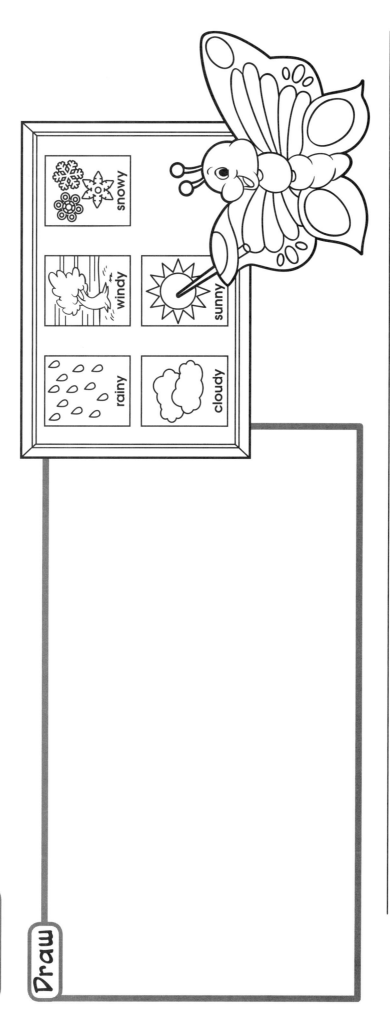

Wonder What is your favorite kind of weather?

Draw

Tell _____

- - - - - - - - - - - -

- - - - - - - - - - - -

Hiding Out

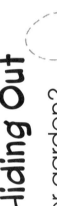

Wonder Who is hiding in the flower garden?

Draw

Tell

_ _ _ _ _ _ _ _ _ _ _ _ _ _ _ _ _ _ _

_____

_____

Name _____

A Vegetable Garden

Wonder What will grow?

Draw

Tell _____
_ _ _ _ _ _ _ _ _ _ _ _ _ _ _ _ _ _ _ _
_____
_ _ _ _ _ _ _ _ _ _ _ _ _ _ _ _ _ _ _ _
_____
_ _ _ _ _ _ _ _ _ _ _ _ _ _ _ _ _ _ _ _

Oh, My!

Wonder What surprised the gardener?

Draw

Tell _____

_____

_____

_____

_____

Name

Happy Plants

Wonder What would your garden look like?

Draw

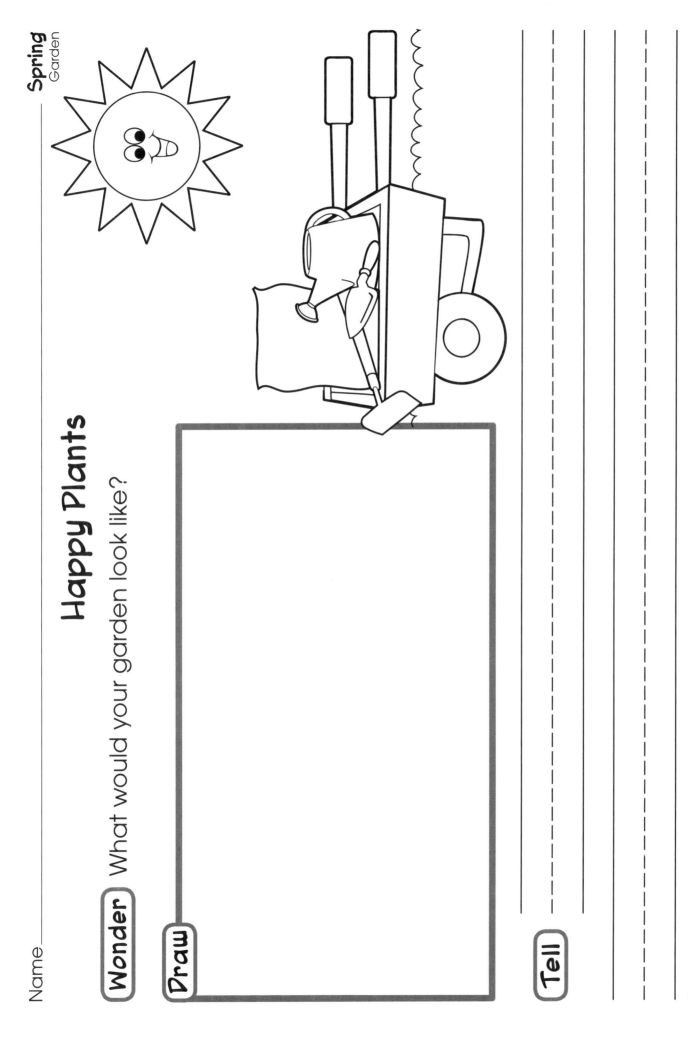

Tell

Wonder, Draw, Tell! • ©The Mailbox® Books • TEC61274

Look Who's Sharing!

Wonder Who will get the carrot?

Draw

Tell
_____
- -
_____
- -
_____
- -
_____

Wonder, Draw, Tell! ©The Mailbox® Books • TEC61274

Great Colors!

Wonder What will the bunny draw?

Draw

Tell

Hop, Hop, Hop!

Wonder Where is the bunny going?

Draw

Tell

A Day at the Pond

Wonder What is on the log?

Draw

Tell _____
_____
_____
_____
_____
_____
_____

Name _____

44

Looking Underwater

Wonder What does the duck see?

Draw

Tell

Name

Sleepy Alligator

Wonder What is happening in the pond?

Draw

Tell

- - - - - - - - - - - - -

Bye-Bye, Frog

Wonder Who will miss the frog?

Draw

Tell

Wonder, Draw, Tell! • ©The Mailbox® Books • TEC61274

Name _____

Looking for a Landing

Wonder What will the ladybug land on?

Draw

Tell

_____
- - - - - - - - - - - -
_____
_____

Wonder, Draw, Tell! • ©The Mailbox® Books • TEC61274

Name

48

Sweet Dreams

Wonder What is the spider dreaming about?

Draw

Tell

Name

Buzz, Buzz!

Wonder Where are the bees going?

Draw

Tell

Pet Bug

Wonder What does the bug look like?

Draw

Tell _____

_____

_____

_____

_____

Wonder, Draw, Tell! • ©The Mailbox® Books • TEC61274

Name _____

Sunny Day

Wonder Who will go to the beach?

Draw

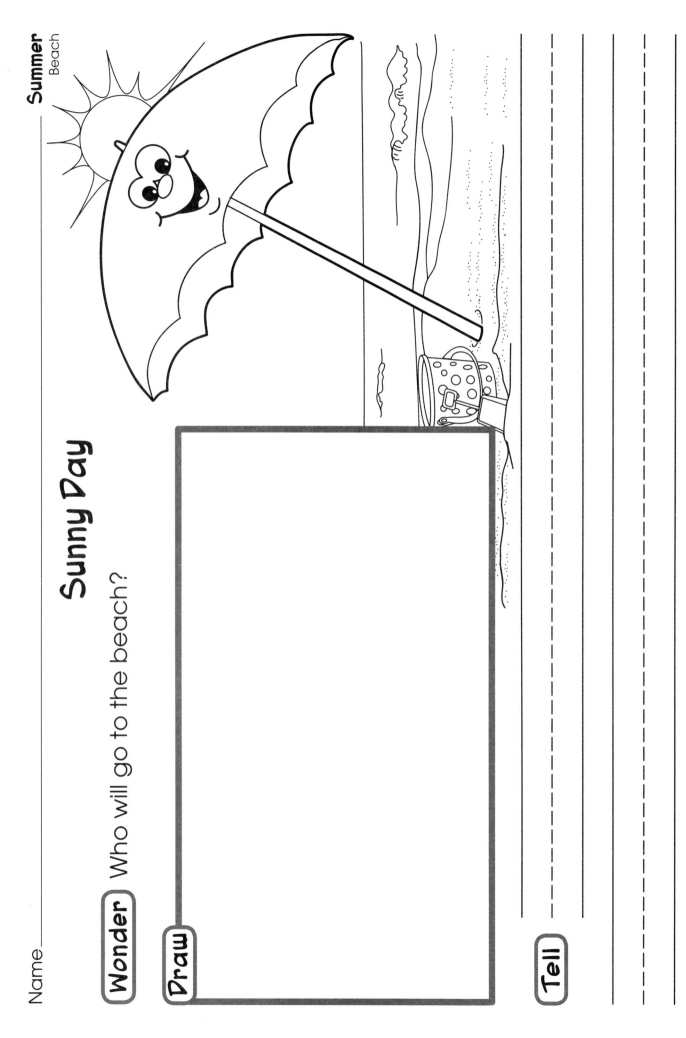

Tell

Surf's Up!

Wonder What will happen next?

Draw

Tell

Wonder, Draw, Tell! • ©The Mailbox® Books • TEC61274

Name

Crab's Castle

Wonder What will the sand castle look like?

Draw

Tell

Wonder, Draw, Tell! • ©The Mailbox® Books • TEC61274

Name

54

Exploring the Ocean

Wonder What does the bird see?

Draw

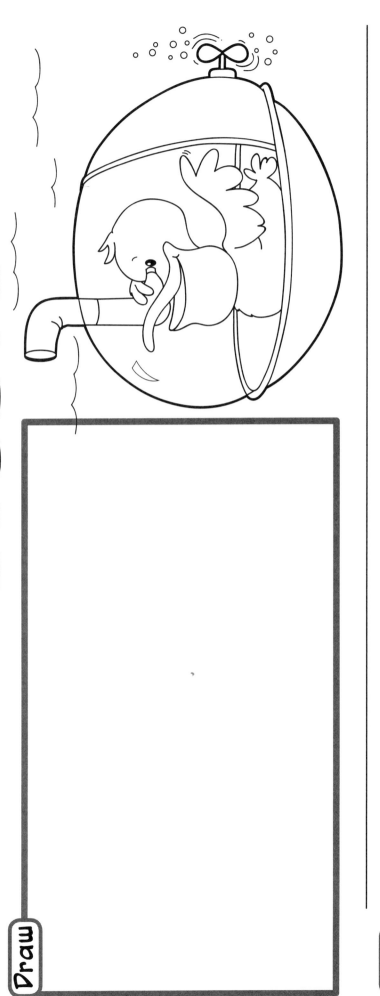

Tell

Name _____

A Stuffed Basket

Wonder What would you pack for a picnic?

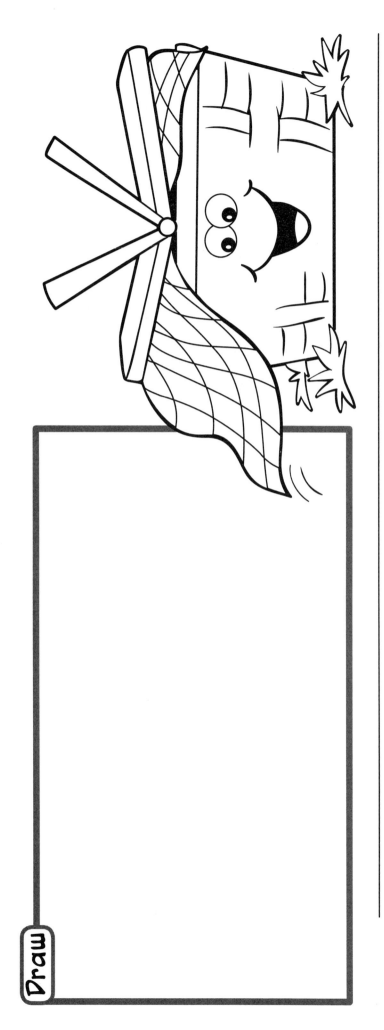

Draw

Tell _____

Wonder, Draw, Tell! • ©The Mailbox® Books • TEC61274

Name

A Picnic in the Park

Wonder Who will come to the picnic?

Draw

Tell

56

All Gone!

Wonder Who ate the watermelon?

Draw

Tell

Ice Cream Truck

Wonder What would you get?

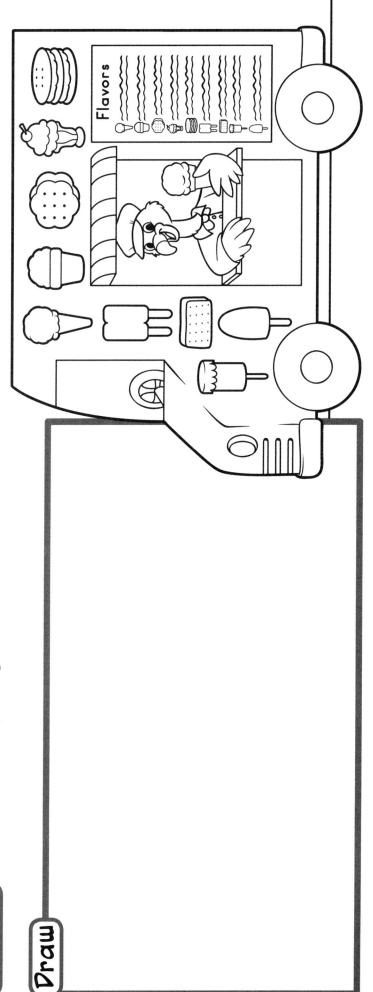

Flavors

Draw

Tell

Yummy Ice Cream

Wonder What did the cow order?

Draw

Specials

Tell

Wonder, Draw, Tell! • ©The Mailbox® Books • TEC61274

Name_____

Oops!

Wonder What will make the dragon feel better?

Draw

Tell _____
_____
_____
_____
_____
_____

Wonder, Draw, Tell! ©The Mailbox® Books • TEC61274

Anytime
Community helpers

Fast Fire Truck!

Wonder What will happen next?

Draw

Tell

A Visit With the Vet

Wonder What will the vet help next?

Draw

Tell _____

_____

_____

_____

_____

_____

_____

Wonder, Draw, Tell! • ©The Mailbox® Books • TEC61274

Thank You, Teacher!

Wonder What does your teacher do to help you?

cat

Draw

Tell

_ _

Ready to Hatch

Wonder What will the dinosaur look like?

Draw

Tell _

_____

_ _

_____

_ _

Looking Around

Wonder What does the dinosaur see?

Draw

Tell _____

_ _ _ _ _ _ _ _ _ _ _ _ _ _ _ _ _ _

_____

Name _____

Time to Learn

Wonder What would a dinosaur do at school?

Draw

Tell

- -

- -

Home, Sweet Home

Wonder What lives on the farm?

Draw

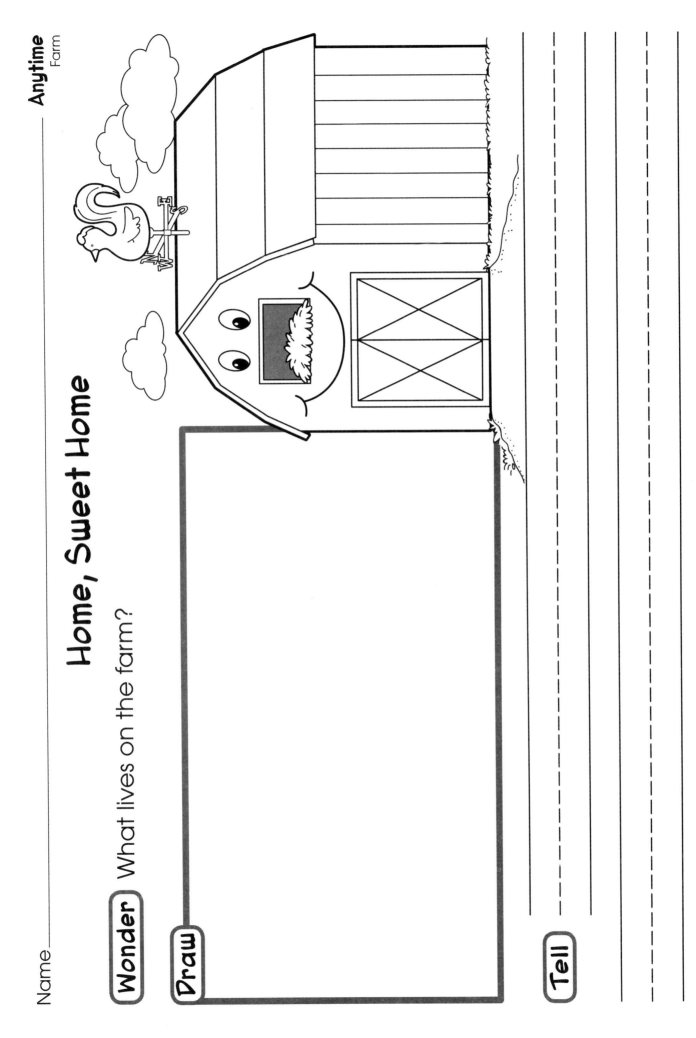

Tell

- - - - - - - - - - - - - -

- - - - - - - - - - - - - -

Hurry!

Wonder Why is the farmer running?

Draw

Tell _ _ _ _ _ _ _ _ _ _ _ _ _ _ _ _ _

Wonder, Draw, Tell! • ©The Mailbox® Books • TEC61274

Hide-and-Seek

Wonder Where are the other chicks?

Draw

Tell

Wonder, Draw, Tell! • ©The Mailbox® Books • TEC61274

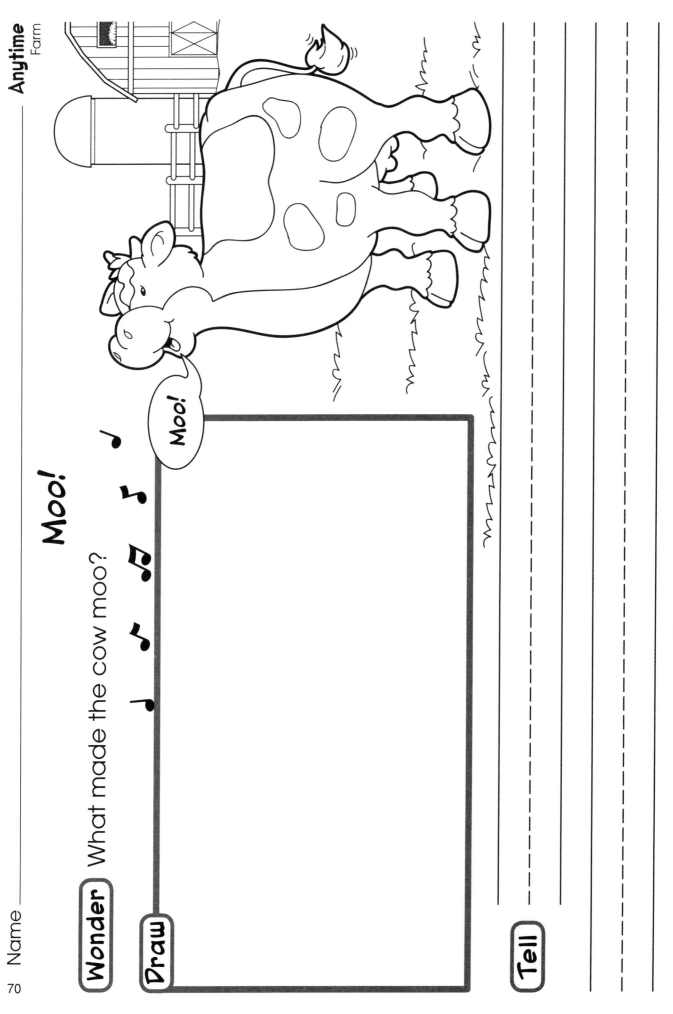

Moo!

Wonder What made the cow moo?

Moo!

Draw

Tell

Woof!

Wonder What is the dog barking at?

Draw

Tell _____

_____

_____

Look Out!

Wonder What surprised the bird?

Draw

Tell

My New Pet

Wonder What pet would **you** get?

Draw

Pet Store

Tell

_____

- - - - - - - - - - - - - - - - - - -

_____

- - - - - - - - - - - - - - - - - - -

_____

- - - - - - - - - - - - - - - - - - -

_____

- - - - - - - - - - - - - - - - - - -

_____

Traveling by Boat

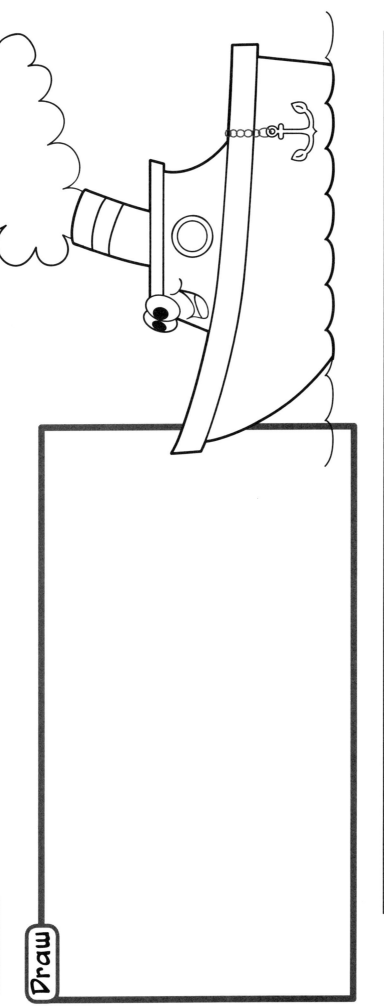

Wonder Where is the boat going?

Draw

Tell

Name

Going Up!

Wonder What will the hippo see?

Draw

Tell

_ _

_ _

_ _

Name

76

Road Trip

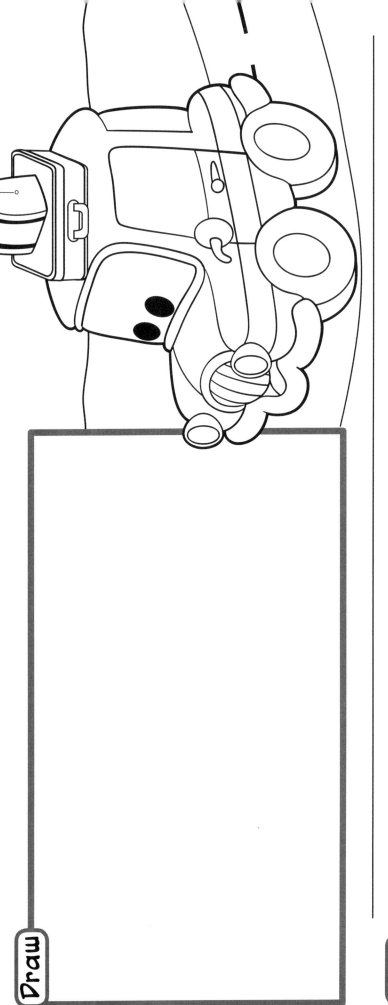

Wonder Who will get in the car?

Draw

Tell

Ready to Go!

Wonder What is your favorite way to travel?

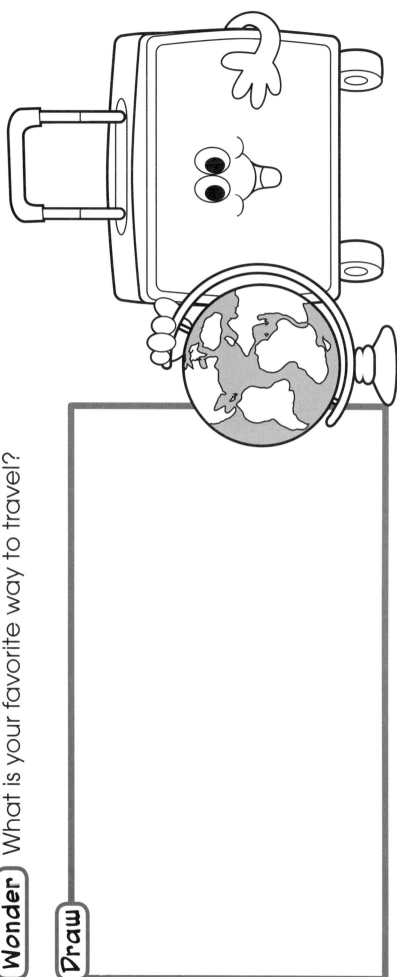

Draw

Tell _____

Wonder, Draw, Tell! • ©The Mailbox® Books • TEC61274

Stolen Key

Wonder What will happen next?

Draw

Tell

A Reason to Smile

Wonder What made the elephant happy?

Draw

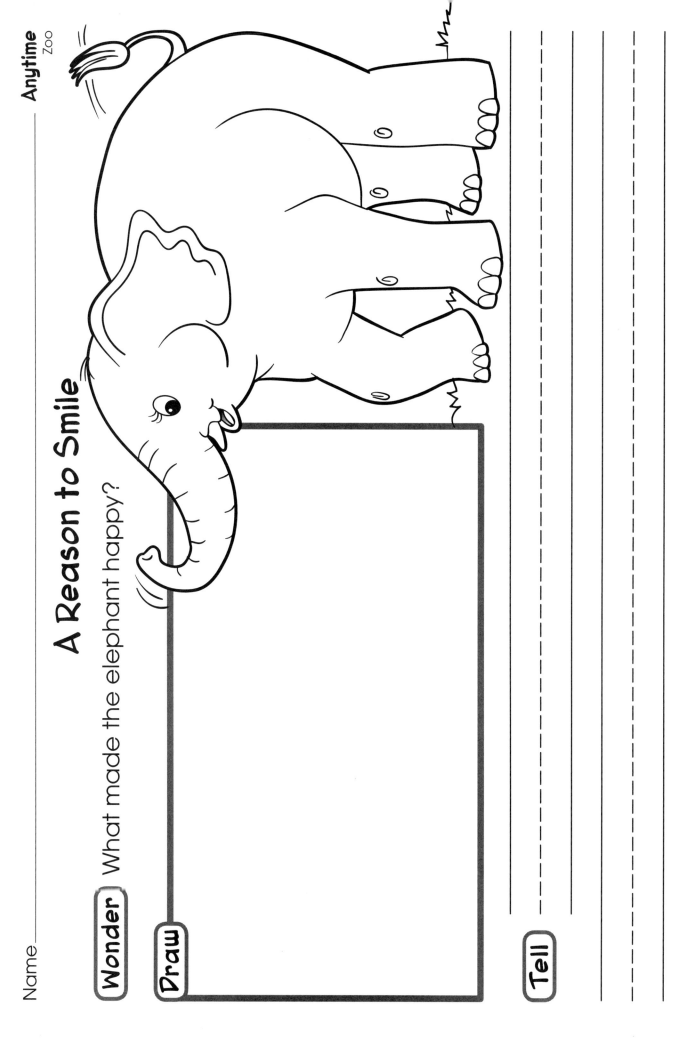

Tell _____

Wonder, Draw, Tell! • ©The Mailbox® Books • TEC61274

Zoo Animals

Wonder What animals would **you** like to see?

Draw

WELCOME to the **ZOO**

Tell _____

_____

_____

_____

_____

_____